Breaking Chains Using Blockchain 2.0

Cryptocurrency for Beginners

(2025 Edition)

Jacob Tadesse, Micheal Duvall and Robert Bazile

Table of Contents

Preface

If you haven't explored cryptocurrency (crypto) by now, you may still be chained to a system designed to keep you broke.

As of 2025, we stand firmly in the creative and decentralized age. Emerging from the disruptive events of the early 2020s, global pandemics, rising inflation, economic disillusionment, a growing number of people are recognizing that traditional financial systems no longer serve everyone equally. The wealth divide has become a full-blown wealth chasm. While Wall Street posts record profits, everyday families, especially Black and Brown households, are drowning in debt, inflation, and diminishing purchasing power. But there is a quiet revolution underway: **digital currency**.

Crypto isn't just a trend anymore. With Bitcoin reaching above $100,000 and nations like El Salvador, Nigeria, and Brazil integrating crypto and CBDCs (Central Bank Digital Currencies) into their economies, the writing is on the wall: **fiat alone is no longer freedom.**

Moore's Law, the idea that technology doubles in capability roughly every two years, remains relevant; but now it applies to *financial* tools too. DeFi (Decentralized Finance), tokenization, AI-powered trading, and blockchain governance are evolving at a breakneck pace. The systems of the past century can't keep up.

This book is a map. It won't drown you in tech speak. Instead, it speaks to you directly, like a friend who's been where you are: frustrated with the paycheck-to-paycheck hustle, skeptical of big banks, tired of being last to know where the real money is moving. So if you're still stuck in the fiat rat race, let this be your wake-up call. And if you already hold crypto, you'll find more tools, insights, and motivation to level up.

Let's break chains. Together.

Introduction

Bitcoin is a digital currency, much like the dollar or pound, but with critical differences. Introduced by the pseudonymous developer Satoshi Nakamoto in 2009, it functions on a peer-to-peer network that allows the direct exchange of value (goods, services, or savings) between individuals, without needing a central authority like a bank or government.

Now, in **2025**, Bitcoin is no longer the fringe idea it once was. It has crossed a $1.5 trillion market cap and consistently trades above **$80,000 USD**. Entire countries, including **El Salvador** and **the Central African Republic**, have adopted it as legal tender. Major fintech platforms and payment giants, from **PayPal and Square** to **Cash App and Stripe**, now integrate Bitcoin and other cryptocurrencies into everyday finance. **BlackRock, Fidelity**, and several other asset managers have launched **Bitcoin ETFs** (Exchange-Traded Funds), signaling full institutional acceptance.

Bitcoin operates on a decentralized network of computers called nodes, which validate and secure transactions using a process called **proof-of-work**. This ensures every transaction is recorded on a public ledger known as the **blockchain**, making Bitcoin highly transparent and censorship-resistant.

While Bitcoin's journey has included extreme volatility and media skepticism, its long-term trend shows increasing adoption, growing use as a hedge against inflation, and a maturing ecosystem of wallets, exchanges, and applications.

More than just digital money, Bitcoin represents a movement; toward sovereignty, privacy, and borderless value exchange. For communities historically excluded from traditional finance, especially Black and Brown populations globally, Bitcoin offers a parallel system where the barriers to entry are far lower, and the potential upside far greater.

So whether you're here because you're curious, cautious, or ready to flip your first satoshi, this chapter; and this book, will walk with you step-by-step.

Let's get started.

Chapter One:

This Decade of Dying Fiat Currencies

As of 2025, the erosion of trust in fiat currencies is no longer a fringe concern, it's front-page news. From soaring national debts to runaway inflation, central banks across the globe are grappling with crises of confidence. The U.S. national debt has surpassed **$35 trillion**, and over 50 countries now experience inflation above **10%**, according to the IMF (International Monetary Fund).

A stark example of collapsing fiat systems was **Lebanon**, where the local currency lost more than **90%** of its value over three years. In **Argentina**, inflation crossed **211%** in 2024. And in **Nigeria**, severe cash shortages drove more citizens into crypto wallets than ever before.

In a significant geopolitical shift, **China** and **Saudi Arabia** have begun settling energy trades in **yuan and gold**, bypassing the U.S. dollar. **BRICS nations** (Brazil, Russia, India, China, South Africa) have accelerated plans for a **blockchain-based alternative reserve system**, challenging the petrodollar status quo. The dollar's supremacy is under siege not just from rivals but from systemic overprinting and debt monetization.

While central banks issue stimulus with digital keystrokes, gold and silver remain time-tested hedges against currency collapse. As of early 2025, gold hovers above **$3,000 per ounce**, and silver is catching up fast, with a gold-to-silver ratio nearing **65:1**;

still well above its historical average (12:1), signaling potential upside for silver.

Meanwhile, **Bitcoin** has entered the mainstream as "digital gold" for a new generation. With its hard-capped supply of 21 million coins, decentralized structure, and resistance to inflation, Bitcoin offers the same scarcity and store-of-value properties as gold, but with added portability and borderless utility.

As the cracks in the fiat system widen, a rising chorus is opting out. Whether through metals, DeFi, or digital assets, people are reclaiming control over their wealth. For those tired of watching their money shrink, crypto isn't just a speculative bet, it's a lifeline.

How Cryptocurrency Works

Cryptocurrency is a form of digital money that uses advanced cryptographic techniques to secure transactions and control the creation of new units. While cryptography dates back to World War II for secure communications, today's cryptocurrency protocols are grounded in modern breakthroughs in blockchain technology and distributed computing.

Unlike traditional banking systems, which rely on centralized institutions like banks or governments, cryptocurrencies operate on **decentralized networks** most commonly built on **blockchains**. These are public, tamper-resistant digital ledgers maintained across thousands of computers globally. This decentralized architecture allows users to send, receive, and store value without needing permission or approval from any central authority.

Cryptocurrencies such as **BTC (Bitcoin)**, **ETH (Ethereum)**, and **SOL (Solana)** are now widely traded across the globe. As of 2025, over **500 million crypto wallets** are in use, and adoption continues to grow, especially in regions like **Latin America, Sub-Saharan Africa, and Southeast Asia**, where access to traditional banking is limited.

How Coins Are Created

The creation of new coins varies by blockchain:

- **Proof-of-Work (PoW)**: Used by Bitcoin, this system rewards miners who solve complex mathematical problems to validate transactions and secure the network.
- **Proof-of-Stake (PoS)**: Now used by Ethereum and many newer blockchains, this method allows users to validate transactions and earn rewards by locking up their tokens.
- **Other Methods**: Some networks use **Delegated Proof-of-Stake (DPoS)** or **Proof-of-History (PoH)** to optimize for speed and scalability.

Wallets and Accessibility

Users can store cryptocurrency in digital wallets, which range from mobile apps like **Trust Wallet** and **MetaMask** to more secure **hardware wallets** like **Ledger** or **Trezor**. Wallets provide a public address (like a bank account number) and a private key (like a password) to control your assets.

Blockchain technology enables **near-instant global transfers**, **low fees**, and **financial access** for the underbanked. It also supports innovations like **NFTs (Non-Funglible Tokens)**, **tokenized assets**, and **DeFi** all of which have become increasingly mainstream.

Responsible Use and Caution

While cryptocurrency offers privacy and autonomy, it can also be misused for illicit activities. In 2024, regulatory bodies like the **SEC**, **FATF**, and **G20** member states introduced stricter compliance requirements around **KYC (Know Your Customer)** and **AML (Anti-Money Laundering)** standards.

To stay safe:

- Use trusted, regulated exchanges.
- Store your private keys securely.
- Avoid "pump and dump" schemes or unsolicited crypto offers.

In the new digital economy, crypto is no longer optional. It's essential knowledge. For anyone seeking financial freedom, understanding how cryptocurrency works is the first step in breaking the chains of outdated money systems.

How to Find Cryptocurrency Predictions

In 2025, staying informed is not just helpful, it's essential. With crypto markets evolving faster than ever, accurate predictions require a blend of data analysis, credible platforms, and community insight.

Here are updated tools and platforms trusted by the global crypto community:

- **TradingView**: Still a top-tier charting tool. In 2025, it includes AI-powered pattern recognition and integrates on-chain data to help forecast price action more reliably. Look for user-generated scripts and trend alerts from verified analysts.
- **DappRadar**: More relevant than ever, DappRadar now tracks metrics across Ethereum, Solana, Polygon, and Layer-2 rollups. It ranks apps by active users, transaction volume, and revenue helping you identify promising projects early.
- **MarketCapOf.com**: This simulation tool allows you to visualize how the market cap of smaller coins might perform if they reached the size of top cryptocurrencies. In 2025, it supports tokenomics inputs, vesting schedules, and real-time liquidity metrics.
- **TokenTerminal**: A favorite among serious DeFi investors. It now offers revenue-based valuations for protocols, comparing fee generation, active wallets, and token holder distributions. Great for identifying undervalued assets based on real usage.
- **Messari & Artemis.xyz** *(New)*: Both platforms now offer institutional-grade dashboards combining

tokenomics, VC investment history, and protocol roadmaps.

- **X (formerly Twitter) & Discord** *(Caution!)*: While not formal prediction tools, social platforms are still vital for early alpha. Just be careful many influencers are paid promoters. Cross-check claims with real data.

2025 Best Practices:

- Avoid influencers promising "10x overnight" gains.
- Use **on-chain data** to verify project health: check daily active users, Total Value Locked (TVL), and treasury holdings.
- Compare predictions across multiple sources. No single platform sees the full picture.

The smartest investors in 2025 treat prediction tools as one piece of the puzzle. Combine technical analysis, on-chain metrics, community sentiment, and macroeconomic context to make informed decisions.

Remember: It's not about being first. It's about being right *enough*, consistently.

Practical Tips for Trading Cryptocurrencies

Start your day informed: Check comprehensive sites like **CoinMarketCap**, **CoinGecko**, or **Artemis** for real-time prices, market sentiment, on-chain activity, and protocol metrics. Pay attention to volume spikes, TVL, and major announcements.

Avoid FOMO (Fear of Missing Out): Don't rush into trending tokens or meme coins. Analyze project fundamentals, recent token unlocks, and liquidity before buying in. In a high-speed market, patience is power.

Diversify: Don't put all your eggs in one chain or asset. Allocate across major tokens (like BTC, ETH, SOL), stablecoins (USDC, USDT, crvUSD), and high-conviction altcoins. Consider including assets from different sectors such as DeFi, gaming, and AI.

Use test accounts or simulators: Platforms like **TradingView Paper Trading** or **Binance Futures Testnet** let you practice strategies before putting real money on the line.

Stay focused: Don't chase every new coin or hype trend. Many "airdrops" or meme tokens have no real utility. Build a watchlist of projects you understand and believe in long term.

Adopt a data-driven strategy: Use tools like **IntoTheBlock**, **Santiment**, or **Token Terminal** to review investor sentiment, active addresses, and developer activity. Combine technical indicators with fundamental metrics.

Invest in real-world use cases: Favor projects solving actual problems like remittances, decentralized storage, identity verification, or AI infrastructure. Use the tech yourself when possible.

Commit to ongoing education: Stay updated on trends, regulations, and emerging technologies like:

- AI-driven trading signal platforms
- Layer 2 scaling (Base, Optimism, zkSync)
- Modular blockchain infrastructure (Celestia, EigenLayer)
- Decentralized perpetuals platforms (dYdX, GMX, Hyperliquid)
- Governance and tokenomics shifts (ve-token models, re-staking)

In 2025, a sharp trader blends caution with curiosity. Track macro trends, read protocol updates, and follow credible analytics. Crypto is 24/7 so your knowledge needs to be as well.

Chapter Two:

Benefits of Cryptocurrency

Fraud Resistance: Transactions are cryptographically secured and recorded on immutable ledgers (blockchains), making them nearly impossible to alter retroactively. In 2025, more platforms use **zero-knowledge proofs** and **multi-sig wallets** to further prevent tampering.

Instant Settlement: Crypto transactions settle in seconds to minutes much faster than traditional financial systems that rely on intermediaries. With the rise of **Layer 2 solutions** like Optimism and Base, transfers are now cheaper and near-instant, even during peak activity.

Low Fees: Especially on scalable networks like **Solana**, **Arbitrum**, or **Polygon**, transaction costs can be less than a penny. This is critical for microtransactions, remittances, and everyday use cases.

User-Controlled Privacy: Users decide how much information to share. Tools like **zk-rollups** and privacy chains (e.g., **Secret Network**, **Iron Fish**) give enhanced privacy without compromising compliance.

Borderless Financial Access: Anyone with a smartphone and internet can receive, send, or store crypto. In countries with high inflation or currency control such as ***Argentina**, **Nigeria**, or* ***Turkey*** crypto provides economic lifelines.

Decentralization: Power is spread across a global network of validators or miners instead of a central bank. This reduces censorship, systemic failure risks, and allows for **community governance** (DAOs) where users have voting rights.

Global Reach: Crypto is accepted by more than **250 million users** and integrated into platforms like **PayPal**, **Cash App**, and **Shopify**. From freelancers in Kenya to artists in Brazil, the tools are finally global.

Understanding these benefits in 2025 is more than theoretical; it's a pathway to self-reliance, especially for those excluded or exploited by traditional systems. Whether you're sending money home, escaping inflation, or building wealth from scratch, crypto gives you options, and power.

Tips for Investing in Cryptocurrency

Treat it like commodities: Crypto behaves more like a volatile commodity than a stable currency. Use technical analysis, dollar-cost averaging (DCA), and risk management tools to trade smartly.

Buy from secure and compliant platforms: Leading platforms in 2025 include **Coinbase**, **Kraken**, **Binance US**, and **Bitstamp**. Look for exchanges that follow **KYC/AML regulations** and offer **cold storage** options.

We're still early for some chains: While Bitcoin and Ethereum are now mainstream, emerging ecosystems like **Celestia**, **Sui**, or

Base are in early phases and may present high-risk, high-reward opportunities.

The market continues to evolve: While the total crypto market cap has surpassed **$3 trillion**, major pullbacks and volatility still occur. Learn to zoom out and identify long-term trends.

Utility and adoption matter most: Invest in tokens that power real applications whether its **stablecoins**, **remittance networks**, **data storage (Filecoin, Arweave)**, or **A.I. / compute infrastructure**.

Understand market cycles: Crypto moves in 3 to 4 year waves. 2025 may be a bullish year due to the post-halving cycle, but always prepare for pullbacks. Follow macro trends, ETF flows, and developer activity.

Problem-solving protocols thrive: Look for projects addressing real pain points like cross-border payments, banking the unbanked, or secure voting. Narratives matter, but real-world utility sustains value.

Fiat conversion is easier than ever: Off-ramping is seamless through apps like **Strike**, **Revolut**, **Coinbase Card**, and **Ramp Network**. You can even use crypto to pay bills or buy groceries with integrated debit cards.

Diversify intentionally: Don't just hold dozens of coins. Mix **blue chips**, **stablecoins**, **growth assets**, and possibly **tokenized real-world assets (RWAs)** like real estate or U.S. Treasury-backed stablecoins.

Vet your sources rigorously: Stick with platforms like **Messari**, **Delphi Digital**, **Bankless**, and **Coin Bureau**. Be cautious of TikTok influencers and anonymous pump groups. Always cross-check advice with on-chain data.

In 2025, investing in crypto is about strategy, not hype. Stay educated, stay decentralized, and protect your keys.

Chapter Three:

Bitcoin as an Investment

Bitcoin continues to serve as a decentralized, global alternative to national currencies and now, more than ever, it is being recognized as a **digital store of value** by both institutional investors and everyday users. Its volatility remains a factor, but it is now traded through **spot Bitcoin ETFs** (approved in the U.S. in 2024), **regulated custodians**, and **retirement accounts**, providing greater legitimacy and access. Large asset managers like **BlackRock**, **Fidelity**, and **ARK Invest** have brought Bitcoin exposure to the mainstream.

You can use Bitcoin for long-term investment, international transfers, or savings protection in inflationary environments. Wallets can be created using secure platforms like **Coinbase**, **Strike**, **River**, or **hardware wallets** like **Ledger** and **Trezor**. In 2025, self-custody is strongly encouraged to avoid centralized exchange failures.

Bitcoin's rise has also paved the way for a new economy from **Bitcoin-native apps** built on the **Lightning Network**, to **Bitcoin-backed loans**, and **Layer 2 DeFi protocols** (e.g., Stacks, Rootstock). These innovations allow users to earn yield, pay bills, or access financial services while staying within the Bitcoin ecosystem.

However, regulation is expanding. Governments worldwide now require **KYC/AML compliance**, and some tax authorities track wallet activity. Before investing, understand your jurisdiction's rules and keep clear records for tax purposes.

Bottom Line:

Bitcoin is no longer just a fringe tech experiment, it's an evolving asset class with growing legitimacy, risks, and potential. Educate yourself, store your keys securely, and think long term.

How Bitcoin Works

To reiterate, Bitcoin is a decentralized digital currency that operates independently of banks or governments. Every transaction is recorded on a public, immutable ledger known as the blockchain. With a **Bitcoin wallet**, users can securely send, receive, and store value without needing traditional financial documentation.

Setting Up a Bitcoin Wallet

In 2025, setting up a Bitcoin wallet is fast and flexible. You can:

- Use mobile apps like **BlueWallet**, **Phoenix**, or **Strike** for easy onboarding.
- Choose **custodial wallets** (Coinbase, Cash App) for convenience.
- Use **non-custodial wallets** (like **MetaMask** or **TrustWallet**) for full control of your private keys.

Upon setup, you receive a **public address** (like an account number) and a **private key** (like a password). With self-custody wallets, you must securely store your **recovery phrase** if lost, access to your funds is gone.

Bitcoin's Role in Payments

Bitcoin isn't just an asset it's used for real-world payments thanks to **Lightning Network**, a fast and low-cost Layer 2 solution.

- Apps like **Strike** and **Wallet of Satoshi** let users send Bitcoin globally, often with fees under 1 cent.
- In countries like **El Salvador**, **Argentina**, and parts of **Africa**, Bitcoin is used daily to buy groceries, pay bills, and save in a stronger currency.

Bitcoin is **pseudonymous**, not fully anonymous. While your name isn't tied to your wallet address, all transactions are public. Tools like **Samourai Wallet** and **Whirlpool** offer privacy enhancements, but privacy laws and KYC regulations apply in most regions.

Bitcoin in Gaming and Gambling

Bitcoin's roots in the online gaming and gambling world are still visible. Platforms like **BC.Game**, **Stake**, and **Rollbit** accept crypto for betting and payouts. However, regulation is stricter now. Many platforms require identity verification, and winnings may be taxed depending on jurisdiction.

Sending Bitcoin: Step-by-Step

To send Bitcoin, you need:

1. Your wallet
2. The recipient's Bitcoin address
3. The amount to send

Confirm all details, especially the **network type** (Bitcoin vs. Lightning). Transactions are irreversible. Once sent, they're recorded permanently on the blockchain.

Bottom Line:

Bitcoin has grown beyond its underground reputation. It's now a critical pillar in the emerging decentralized economy. Whether you're using it to hedge against inflation, send money abroad, or pay for everyday items, understanding how Bitcoin works is essential in 2025.

Cryptocurrency Exchanges

Cryptocurrency exchanges are digital platforms that allow users to buy, sell, and trade crypto assets such as **Bitcoin (BTC)**, **Ethereum (ETH)**, and thousands of altcoins and tokens. As of 2025, exchanges have become more sophisticated and regulated, offering better security, user experience, and global access.

There are two main types of exchanges:

- **Centralized Exchanges (CEXs)**: These include platforms like **Coinbase**, **Kraken**, **Binance**, and **Bybit**, where the company holds custody of your funds and matches buyers and sellers.

- **Decentralized Exchanges (DEXs)**: These run on blockchain protocols without intermediaries. Examples include **Uniswap**, **dYdX**, **SushiSwap**, and **Jupiter** (on Solana). You retain full control of your crypto, and trades are peer-to-peer.

Use **trusted, audited platforms** especially when starting out. In 2022 - 2023, events like the **FTX collapse** taught users to prioritize transparency and security. Most leading platforms now publish **Proof-of-Reserves** reports and support **2FA and cold wallet storage**.

⚠️ **Note**: Transactions on most blockchains are irreversible. Always verify the recipient address, network (e.g., Ethereum vs. Arbitrum), and token type before sending.

Exchange Trends in 2025:

- Many exchanges now support **instant fiat on-ramps** via Apple Pay, debit cards, or bank transfers.
- KYC (Know Your Customer) is now standard for most CEXs due to global regulations.
- Advanced DEXs support **limit orders**, **derivatives**, and **cross-chain swaps** using bridges or liquidity hubs like **THORChain**.

While mainstream adoption has improved with apps like **Robinhood** and **PayPal** integrating crypto, many merchants and institutions still hesitate due to regulatory uncertainty. Still, user ownership and usage have surpassed **500 million wallets globally**, and the pace of adoption continues to grow.

Crypto exchanges are your gateway but make sure you walk through them with caution, knowledge, and a wallet you control.

Drawbacks of Cryptocurrency

Despite its transformative potential, cryptocurrency still presents notable challenges in 2025. Here's what every new investor should consider:

- **Volatility**: Crypto markets remain highly volatile. Even top assets like Bitcoin and Ethereum can swing 10-30% in a matter of days. Meme coins and low-cap tokens are even riskier. Always invest what you can afford to lose.
- **Tech Maturity Gaps**: While many Layer 1 and Layer 2 platforms have matured, others especially experimental chains or DeFi protocols can still suffer from bugs, downtime, or exploit vulnerabilities. Audits help, but they're not a guarantee.
- **Regulatory Flux**: In 2025, crypto regulation is rapidly evolving. Some countries offer clarity (e.g., Singapore, UAE), while others remain ambiguous or outright hostile. In the U.S., tax treatment is strict, and KYC/AML enforcement is expanding.
- **Security Risks**: Rug pulls, phishing attacks, bridge exploits, and exchange collapses are still happening. In 2023 alone, over **$2 billion** was lost to DeFi hacks. If

you don't control your private keys, you don't control your crypto.

- **Limited Everyday Usage**: Despite growth in adoption, crypto isn't universally accepted. While some merchants, platforms, and fintechs support payments in USDC or BTC, most daily transactions (rent, groceries, medical bills) still rely on fiat.

Bottom Line:

Crypto is powerful but it's not perfect. Treat it like any financial tool: with education, caution, and a long-term mindset. Know the risks, manage them smartly, and never chase gains without a plan.

Mining of Bitcoin Cash - BCH

Mining is the process of verifying transactions and securing blockchain networks through cryptographic computations. For **Bitcoin Cash (BCH)**, a fork of Bitcoin launched in 2017, the goal has always been to offer **larger block sizes**, enabling faster and cheaper transactions compared to Bitcoin's original protocol.

How BCH Mining Works in 2025

Miners use computing power to solve complex mathematical puzzles (proof-of-work). When a valid block is found, the miner receives a reward in BCH, along with transaction fees from the confirmed transactions in that block. In 2025, BCH's block reward stands at **3.125 BCH**, following the most recent halving event.

BCH uses the same SHA-256 hashing algorithm as Bitcoin, meaning it competes for the same global pool of miners. As of this year, **Bitcoin Cash represents a much smaller percentage of total network hash rate**, but continues to attract miners interested in its lower difficulty adjustments and faster block propagation.

Mining Pools and Profitability

- Most miners join **mining pools** like ViaBTC or Antpool to increase their chances of earning rewards.
- Profitability still depends heavily on **electricity cost**, **hardware efficiency (ASICs like Antminer S19 XP)**, **pool fees**, and **market price volatility**.
- BCH's block size limit of **32MB** allows for higher transaction throughput, but block space is not always fully utilized.

2025 Developments

- **Smart contract support** via CashTokens is gaining traction, allowing decentralized apps (dApps) to be built directly on BCH.
- BCH developers continue to push for on-chain scaling rather than adopting Layer 2 solutions like Bitcoin's Lightning Network.
- Community governance and funding are managed through the **Flipstarter** ecosystem.

Bottom Line:

While Bitcoin Cash doesn't have the same mainstream adoption or developer activity as Bitcoin or Ethereum, it remains a viable project for miners who prioritize low fees, fast confirmation times, and scalable on-chain transactions. However, prospective miners should weigh profitability against hardware costs, market trends, and network competition.

Chapter Four:

Understanding Blockchain

Blockchain is a decentralized technology that securely stores digital information in immutable blocks. Originally built to support **Bitcoin**, blockchain has evolved into a foundational layer for Web3, powering everything from financial applications to gaming, identity, and AI.

Each block contains a list of verified transactions and a unique cryptographic hash that links it to the previous block. This chain of blocks creates a public, tamper-resistant ledger that is maintained by a distributed network of computers (nodes). Because data is decentralized and cryptographically secured, altering a single transaction would require re-mining all subsequent blocks on most of the network, a near-impossible task.

Blockchain provides:

- **Transparency**: All transactions are visible and verifiable by anyone.
- **Security**: Strong encryption and distributed consensus reduce hacking risk.
- **Decentralization**: No single point of control or failure.
- **Trustless interactions**: Users don't need to trust a central party, only the protocol.

What's New in 2025:

- **Modular blockchains** like **Celestia** and **EigenLayer** allow developers to build scalable apps with shared security.
- **Zero-knowledge proofs (ZKPs)** enhance privacy while keeping blockchains compliant.
- **Blockchain AI integrations** are growing used for on-chain data verification, model tracking, and decentralized AI coordination.
- **Real-world asset (RWA) tokenization** is bringing real estate, stocks, and even U.S. Treasuries on-chain.

Industries applying blockchain in 2025 include:

- **Healthcare** (data integrity, patient privacy)
- **Finance** (tokenized assets, on-chain compliance)
- **Logistics** (real-time tracking, fraud reduction)
- **Education** (credential verification, lifelong learning records)

Blockchain is no longer just for crypto traders. It's a public utility layer reshaping digital ownership, identity, and coordination. Whether you're investing or building, understanding blockchain is your gateway to the decentralized world.

Blockchain in Supply Chains

In 2025, blockchain is no longer a pilot project in logistics, it's an enterprise-grade solution being implemented across global supply chains. Companies like **Maersk**, **Walmart**, **BHP**, **FedEx**, and **Nestlé** use blockchain platforms such as **IBM Food Trust**, **VeChain**, and **TradeLens** to improve visibility, accountability, and speed.

Here are some of the key benefits that have matured in the past few years:

- **Real-time tracking**: Shipments can be tracked live from origin to destination using blockchain-integrated IoT devices.
- **Immutable document verification**: Bills of lading, certificates of origin, and customs clearances are recorded on-chain, eliminating paper trails and manual checks.
- **Fraud reduction and anti-counterfeiting**: Unique digital fingerprints (hashes) and tokenized assets ensure authenticity in luxury goods, pharmaceuticals, and food logistics.
- **Improved transparency**: All stakeholders suppliers, regulators, retailers, and consumers can verify a product's journey across the supply chain with blockchain-backed provenance data.

What's New in 2025:

- **Carbon tracking and ESG reporting**: Blockchain helps verify sustainability claims with on-chain data showing emissions, sourcing, and compliance.
- **Smart contracts for auto-payments**: Delivery milestones can now trigger instant payments through embedded logic, reducing delays and disputes.

- **Integration with AI and IoT**: Sensors feed real-time data (temperature, humidity, delays) into blockchain networks, while AI flags anomalies and optimizes routes.

Blockchain brings accountability to global trade. For communities and entrepreneurs aiming to build ethical, transparent, and resilient businesses, blockchain-backed supply chain solutions aren't just smart, they're necessary.

Central Bank Digital Currency (CBDC) Initiatives

Since their early pilots in 2019, Central Bank Digital Currencies (CBDCs) have made major strides. As of 2025, over **130 countries** are actively researching or developing CBDCs, with more than **20 nations** having launched pilot programs or full deployments.

Some key highlights:

- **Eastern Caribbean**: The DCash pilot continues expanding, supporting cross-border settlements between island economies.
- **China**: The Digital Yuan (e-CNY) is now used in multiple cities and integrated with apps like WeChat and Alipay. It is the most advanced large-scale CBDC to date.

- **Nigeria**: The eNaira, Africa's first official CBDC, has expanded into retail use cases like merchant payments and government disbursements.
- **Brazil**: The Drex project is in advanced testing, focusing on tokenized bank deposits and wholesale settlement.
- **European Central Bank (ECB)**: The Digital Euro is in its design phase, with public consultations emphasizing privacy and offline payment functionality.
- **United States**: While the Fed has not launched a retail CBDC, research into a digital dollar continues through Project Hamilton and private-public collaborations.

What This Means for You:

CBDCs represent a major shift in how governments think about money. They are designed to improve financial inclusion, reduce settlement friction, and give central banks better tools for monetary policy. However, critics raise concerns about surveillance and financial control.

As blockchain based finance expands, CBDCs offer another signal that the future of money is digital. While not permissionless like Bitcoin or Ethereum, they reinforce blockchain's legitimacy and their rise demands that we stay informed about how power, privacy, and access will be managed in the next era of currency.

Conclusion:

The time to understand and act on cryptocurrency is **no longer in the future, it's now**. With over **500 million global crypto users**, Bitcoin ETFs trading on Wall Street, and central banks launching digital currencies, the decentralized era is fully underway.

Blockchain is being integrated into healthcare, finance, education, and even art. Crypto is paying wages, funding protests, and helping families survive hyperinflation. Whether it's a stablecoin saving a grandmother's retirement in Argentina or an artist in Atlanta minting an NFT to bypass exploitative middlemen, blockchain is **breaking chains** worldwide.

If you're reading this, you're already ahead. The key now is action. Open a wallet. Join a community. Study a new protocol. Help your family get on the blockchain. This space belongs to the bold, the curious, and the committed.

Cryptocurrency and blockchain are not just trends, they are **infrastructure for financial freedom**. Take what you've learned and keep building. Education is still the most valuable coin you can carry into this new age. And with it, you can mint your own future.

www.ingramcontent.com/pod-product-compliance
Lightning Source LLC
LaVergne TN
LVHW101618210926
848480LV00009B/824

9798218901660